Playing Blackjack Like an Engineer

David A. Janover, PE

Copyright

Playing Blackjack Like an Engineer

© 2024 David A. Janover, P.E.

First Edition: August, 2024

ISBN: 9798334622135

Author: David A. Janover, P.E.

Disclaimer: This book is intended for informational and educational purposes only. The author and publisher do not guarantee the accuracy, completeness, or timeliness of the information contained within and shall not be liable for any errors, omissions, or any losses, injuries, or damages arising from its use. The strategies discussed in this book are based on the author's experience and knowledge and may not be suitable for all readers. Readers are encouraged to consult with a professional before engaging in gambling activities.

Contact Information: For inquiries or feedback, please contact the author at djanover1@gmail.com

Printed in the United States of America.

TABLE OF CONTENTS

Introduction

Welcome and Overview

Welcome to "Playing Blackjack Like an Engineer." In this book, we'll explore the fascinating world of Blackjack through the lens of engineering principles. Whether you are an experienced player looking to refine your strategies or a newcomer eager to learn, this book will equip you with the tools and knowledge to play Blackjack with the precision and analytical approach of an engineer.

Blackjack is not just a game of chance; it is a game of skill, strategy, and mathematics. By understanding the underlying principles and applying logical strategies, you can significantly improve your odds of winning. This book will guide you through the basics of the game, delve into advanced strategies, and demonstrate how engineering concepts can be applied to optimize your play.

The Engineer's Approach to Games

Engineers are known for their analytical thinking, problem-solving skills, and systematic approach to challenges. When applied to Blackjack, these qualities can improve your chances of winning at the table. This book will help you learn how to:

- Analyze the game using probability and statistics
- Develop and optimize strategies based on mathematical models
- Manage risk and bankroll effectively

By the end of this book, you will have a comprehensive understanding of Blackjack and the tools to play like an engineer.

Parallels Between Engineering and Blackjack

Drawing parallels between engineering and Blackjack can provide a clear understanding of how the skills and approaches in one field can be applied to another. Here are some key analogies:

Learning Theories and Applying Them: In engineering, students learn proven theories and concepts, which are then applied to real-world projects. Similarly, in Blackjack, the player learns the concepts, rules of the game, and the theory behind basic strategy, which are then applied during real-world gameplay at the Blackjack table.

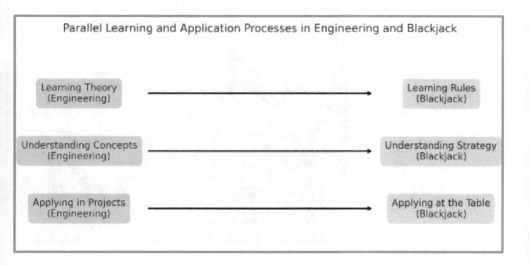

Parallel Learning and Application Processes in Engineering and Blackjack

Learning Theory (Engineering) ——————→ Learning Rules (Blackjack)

Understanding Concepts (Engineering) ——————→ Understanding Strategy (Blackjack)

Applying in Projects (Engineering) ——————→ Applying at the Table (Blackjack)

Project Management and Money Management: In engineering project management, the engineer must monitor the project budget, ensuring that resources are allocated effectively, and costs are controlled. Similarly, a successful Blackjack player must employ money management principles to monitor and manage their bankroll, ensuring they have enough funds to stay in the game and take advantage of profitable situations.

Optimization Techniques: Engineers use optimization techniques to make systems more efficient and effective. In Blackjack, players use optimization strategies to make the best possible decisions based on the cards in play and the dealer's upcard, thereby maximizing their expected value (EV).

Risk Management: Engineering projects often involve risk management to mitigate potential issues that could impact the project's success. Blackjack players also need to manage risk by understanding the probabilities of different outcomes and making decisions that minimize the risk of losing while maximizing the potential for winning.

Data Analysis and Decision Making: Engineers rely on data analysis to inform their decisions and improve project outcomes. In Blackjack, players can use statistical analysis and probability to guide their decisions, making informed choices that improve their chances of winning.

By understanding these parallels, you can leverage your engineering mindset to approach Blackjack systematically and strategically, enhancing your gameplay and increasing your chances of success.

Objective of the Book

The objective of this book is to provide you with a solid foundation in Blackjack by discussing Basic Strategy and showing you how to apply engineering principles to enhance your gameplay. Whether you're playing for fun or aiming to win big, the knowledge and techniques in this book will help you achieve your goals. Additionally, we will discuss bankroll management strategies and betting techniques later in the book, ensuring you are equipped with comprehensive skills for successful play.

Chapter 1: Basics of Blackjack

Understanding the Game

History of Blackjack

Blackjack, also known as 21, has a rich history that dates back to the 17th century. The game is believed to have originated in French casinos around 1700, where it was called "Vingt-et-Un," which means 21. It gained popularity in the United States in the early 1800s, and over time, various rule modifications and strategies were developed, leading to the modern version of Blackjack we know today.

Basic Rules and Terminology

Blackjack is a card game played between one or more players and a dealer. The objective is to have a hand value closer to 21 than the dealer's hand without exceeding 21. Here are the key terms and rules:

- **Hit**: Request an additional card from the dealer.
- **Stand**: Keep your current hand and end your turn.
- **Double Down**: Double your initial bet and receive exactly one more card.

- **Split**: If you have two cards of the same value, you can split them into two separate hands, each with its own bet.
- **Bust**: Exceed a hand value of 21, resulting in an automatic loss.
- **Push**: A tie between the player and the dealer, resulting in no win or loss.

Card Values and the Objective

- Number cards (2-10) are worth their face value.
- Face cards (Jack, Queen, King) are worth 10 points each.
- Aces can be worth 1 or 11 points, depending on which value is more favorable for the hand.

The goal is to have a hand value as close to 21 as possible without going over. If your hand exceeds 21, you bust and lose the bet.

The Blackjack Table Layout and Equipment

A standard Blackjack table seats multiple players and features a semi-circular layout. The dealer stands behind the table, facing the players. The table includes designated areas for placing bets, the dealer's shoe (which holds the decks of cards), and a discard tray for used cards.

Role of the Dealer

The dealer plays a crucial role in Blackjack. They are responsible for shuffling and dealing the cards, managing bets, and enforcing the rules of the game. The dealer must follow strict guidelines for their actions, which include hitting on 16 or less and standing on 17 or more. Understanding the dealer's role and behavior is essential for developing effective strategies.

Chapter 2: Probability and Statistics

Fundamentals of Probability

Basic Probability Concepts

- **Probability**: The likelihood of an event happening, expressed as a fraction or percentage.
- **Independent Events**: Events where the outcome of one does not affect the outcome of another.
- **Deck Composition**: Understanding the makeup of a standard 52-card deck and how it affects probabilities.

Application in Blackjack

- **Single Deck Probability**: At the onset of a single-deck game, the probabilities of drawing specific cards are straightforward. For example, the probability of drawing an Ace from a fresh deck is 4 out of 52 (since there are 4 Aces in a fresh deck), which simplifies to approximately 7.69%.
- **Multi-Deck Probability**: In games with multiple decks (such as 6 or 8 decks), the probabilities as the game progresses are slightly different – while the number of each card type increases proportionally, the overall deck size also increases.

Probability of Drawing a Card with a Value of 10

In Blackjack, cards with a value of 10 include the Tens, Jacks, Queens, and Kings. There are 16 such cards in a standard 52-card deck.

- **Single Deck**: There are 16 cards with a value of 10 in a 52-card deck.
- **Six Decks**: There are 96 cards with a value of 10 in a 312-card deck (6 decks).
- **Eight Decks**: There are 128 cards with a value of 10 in a 416-card deck (8 decks).

Here is a table showing the probability of drawing a 10-value card (10, Jack, Queen, or King) from a single deck, a 6-deck shoe, and an 8-deck shoe:

Deck Type	Cards with Value of 10	Total Cards	Probability of Drawing a 10 (%)
Single Deck	16	52	30.77%
6-Deck Shoe	96	312	30.77%
8-Deck Shoe	128	416	30.77%

The probability of drawing a 10-value card remains consistent across different deck configurations at approximately 30.77%.

This table helps to illustrate that regardless of the number of decks used, the probability of drawing a card with a value of 10 remains constant, forming a key part of the strategic decisions in Blackjack.

The probability of drawing a card with a value of 10 is higher than that of drawing any other specific card value because there are more 10-valued cards in the deck.

Now, for the single and multiple deck scenarios, let's assume that the first card chosen is a card with a value of 10. Comparing the probabilities of choosing another card immediately thereafter having a value of 10 is shown below:

Deck Type	Remaining 10s	Remaining Cards	Probability of Immediately Drawing Another 10 (%)
Single Deck	15	51	29.41%
6-Deck Shoe	95	311	30.55%
8-Deck Shoe	127	415	30.60%

This table demonstrates that for a single deck, the probability of immediately drawing a second 10-value card slightly decreases after one 10 has already been drawn (from 30.77% to 29.41%, a decrease of 1.36%). For multi-deck games, there is less change in the probability of drawing a second 10-value card (-0.22% for the 6-deck shoe and -0.17% for the 8-deck shoe). This is a crucial aspect to consider when making strategic decisions in Blackjack.

Comparison and Strategic Implications

- **Single Deck**: Easier to track cards and predict probabilities after each draw, providing a slight edge to skilled players.
- **Multi-Deck**: More cards in play make it harder to track effectively, and the impact of removing any single card type is less pronounced.

Summary

Understanding the probabilities in Blackjack, whether using a single deck or multiple decks, is crucial for making informed decisions. While the basic probabilities remain consistent, the complexity and strategic implications vary with the number of decks in play. ***Notably, the probability of drawing a card with a value of 10 is higher than that of drawing any other specific card value, which is a key factor in Blackjack strategy.*** This knowledge forms the foundation for basic and advanced strategies, and ultimately, effective gameplay.

Statistical Analysis
Expected Value (EV) in Blackjack

Definition and Importance

Expected Value (EV) is a fundamental concept in probability and statistics, and it plays a crucial role in Blackjack strategy. EV represents the average amount one can expect to win or lose per bet if the same bet were placed repeatedly over a long period. In Blackjack, understanding EV helps players make informed decisions about whether to hit, stand, double down, split or surrender based on the potential long-term outcomes of their actions.

Calculation of Expected Value

The formula for calculating EV is straightforward:

EV = (Probability of Winning × Amount Won) – (Probability of Losing × Amount Lost)

This formula takes into account the probability of each possible outcome and the amount of money won or lost in each scenario.

Example: Calculating EV for a Specific Hand

Let's consider an example to illustrate how EV is calculated in Blackjack.

Scenario: You have a hand totaling 11, and you are considering whether to hit or double down. The dealer's upcard is a 6.

17

1. **Calculating EV for Hitting**
   - **Probability of Winning**: This depends on the remaining cards in the deck and the dealer's potential hand outcomes. For simplicity, let's assume a 75% chance of winning if you hit.
   - **Amount Won**: Assuming you bet $10, the amount won if you beat the dealer is $10.
   - **Probability of Losing**: The probability of losing is the complement of the probability of winning, which is 25%.
   - **Amount Lost**: If you lose, you lose your $10 bet.

Using the EV formula: $EV_{Hit} = (0.75 \times 10) - (0.25 \times 10) = 7.5 - 2.5 = 5$

The expected value of hitting with a total of 11 against a dealer's 6 is $5.

2. **Calculating EV for Doubling Down**
   - **Probability of Winning**: When doubling down, you receive only one additional card. Assume a 70% chance of winning in this case.
   - **Amount Won**: Since you double your bet, the amount won if you beat the dealer is $20.
   - **Probability of Losing**: The probability of losing is the complement, which is 30%.
   - **Amount Lost**: If you lose, you lose your doubled $20 bet.

Using the EV formula: $EV_{Double} = (0.70 \times 20) - (0.30 \times 20) = 14 - 6 = 8$

The expected value of doubling down with a total of 11 against a dealer's 6 is $8.

18

In this example, doubling down has a higher expected value than hitting, so it would be the optimal decision.

Factors Affecting Expected Value

1. **Card Probabilities**: The composition of the remaining deck affects the probabilities of drawing certain cards, influencing the EV of different actions.
2. **Dealer's Upcard**: The dealer's visible card provides information about the dealer's potential hand, impacting the EV of the player's choices.
3. **Number of Decks**: The number of decks in play can slightly alter probabilities and, consequently, the EV of various decisions.
4. **House Rules**: Rules such as whether the dealer hits or stands on soft 17, and the availability of doubling down after splitting, can affect EV calculations.

Using Expected Value in Strategy

Basic Strategy, for which we take a deep dive in Chapter 3, is meticulously designed to maximize the expected value (EV) of each decision a player makes, based on the dealer's upcard and the player's hand. Basic Strategy is derived from extensive simulations involving millions of hands of Blackjack. Each possible scenario was analyzed using these simulations to determine the optimal move—whether to hit, stand, split, double down or surrender — that offers the highest EV for the player.

The goal of these simulations is to identify the statistically best decisions for every possible combination of player hand and dealer upcard. By following Basic Strategy, players can effectively minimize the house edge, which is the casino's built-in advantage over the players. This strategy ensures that players are making the most statistically sound decisions, thereby increasing their chances of winning in the long run.

These simulations account for various game conditions and deck compositions, making Basic Strategy a robust and reliable approach for both single-deck and multi-deck games. The extensive data from these simulations highlight that the optimal plays in Blackjack are not based on intuition, but on rigorous statistical analysis. As a result, Basic Strategy empowers players to reduce their losses and maximize their winnings by adhering to mathematically proven guidelines, ultimately making their gameplay more strategic and informed.

The goal of this book is not just to teach you to memorize the basic strategy chart for Blackjack, but to educate you on the underlying principles of basic strategy. By understanding what basic strategy really is and learning how to read each hand, you will instinctively know how to react in any given situation. This approach ensures that you do not need to rely on the basic strategy chart as a crutch. Instead with practice, you will develop a deep comprehension of the game, allowing you to make optimal decisions with confidence and ease, regardless of the circumstances at the table.

A basic strategy chart, which provides the optimal play for each hand based on the dealer's upcard, is derived from EV calculations, and is provided in Chapter 3. Advanced players may also use EV to inform decisions in card counting[1], where the changing composition of the deck provides additional information to adjust their strategy and betting.

Action and Reaction in Blackjack

In engineering, Newton's Third Law of Motion states that for every action, there is an equal and opposite reaction. This principle essentially applies to Blackjack as well. Knowing that the odds of the next card being a 10-value card are higher than for any other value, we can strategically apply this knowledge to the game. When we see the dealer's upcard as a 5 or 6 (the action), our reaction as player should be to assume that the next card drawn will likely be a 10-value card. This would give the dealer a hand total of 15 or 16, requiring them to hit again. Given the odds, it is favorable for the dealer to draw a subsequent card valued at 7 or higher, which would bust their hand. This action-reaction framework is the cornerstone of Blackjack's basic strategy, guiding players to make the most favorable decisions based on the situation at hand. Other scenarios will be

---

[1] **Card counting** is a strategy used in Blackjack to track the ratio of high cards to low cards remaining in the deck. By keeping a running count, players can estimate the likelihood of drawing high-value cards, which can inform their betting and playing decisions. While card counting can significantly improve a player's odds, it requires substantial practice, concentration, and often a good understanding of mathematical principles. However, this book does not cover card counting techniques. Instead, it focuses on the fundamental strategies and principles of Blackjack that are essential for both novice and intermediate players. For those interested in card counting, numerous specialized resources and books are available.

discussed later in this book, but this principle drives the basic strategy, helping players maximize their chances of winning.

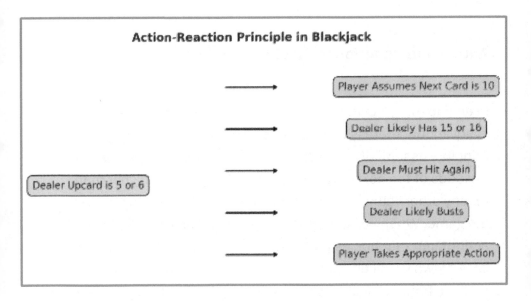

Action-Reaction Principle in Blackjack

Dealer Upcard is 5 or 6

→ Player Assumes Next Card is 10

→ Dealer Likely Has 15 or 16

→ Dealer Must Hit Again

→ Dealer Likely Busts

→ Player Takes Appropriate Action

Conclusion

Understanding and applying the concept of expected value is essential for successful Blackjack play. By evaluating the EV of different actions, players can make informed decisions that maximize their chances of winning over the long term. This analytical approach, grounded in probability and statistics, establishes the framework of Basic Strategy, and is a key aspect of playing Blackjack like an engineer.

Chapter 3: Basic Strategy

Introduction to Basic Strategy

Basic Strategy Overview

- **Definition**: Basic Strategy is a set of guidelines that tells you the best possible move to make in any given Blackjack situation based on the player's hand and the dealer's upcard.
- **Goal**: The goal of Basic Strategy is to minimize the house edge and maximize the player's chances of winning by making the most statistically favorable decisions.

Fundamentals of Basic Strategy

- **Card Values**: Understand the values of different cards (2-10, Jacks, Queens, Kings, and Aces).
- **Hard Hands vs. Soft Hands**: Know the difference between hard hands (without an Ace or with an Ace valued as 1) and soft hands (with an Ace valued as 11).

Categories of Hands

In Blackjack, players can be faced with three distinct categories of hands, each requiring a different strategic approach. The first category is a **Hard Hand**, which is a hand without an Ace or with an Ace valued as 1. The second category is a **Soft Hand**, which includes an Ace counted as 11 along with another card, providing flexibility in how the hand's total value is calculated. The third category is a **Pair**, which consists of two cards of the same value, giving the player the option to split the hand into two separate hands. Understanding these categories is crucial for applying the correct basic strategy and making optimal decisions during gameplay.

Basic Strategy Chart
Using the Chart

- **How to Read**: The basic strategy chart is typically read by finding the player's hand on the left side and the dealer's upcard along the top. The intersection gives the recommended action.
- **Key Actions**:
    - **H**: Hit
    - **S**: Stand
    - **D**: Double Down
    - **T**: Split
    - **X**: Surrender

As mentioned above, there are three (3) categories of hands that the player can be faced with (a **Hard Hand**, a **Soft Hand** and a **Pair**).

The Basic Strategy Chart is shown below, with a detailed explanation of the chart broken down by the type of hand. The upper rows show the Hard Hands, the middle rows show the Soft Hands and the bottom rows show the Pairs.

BASIC STRATEGY CHART

	HIT	STAND		DOUBLE			SPLIT		SURRENDER		
	2	3	4	5	6	7	8	9	10	A	← Dealer's Upcard
17+	S	S	S	S	S	S	S	S	S	S	
16	S	S	S	S	S	H	H	X	X	X	
15	S	S	S	S	S	H	H	H	X	H	
14	S	S	S	S	S	H	H	H	H	H	
13	S	S	S	S	S	H	H	H	H	H	
12	H	H	S	S	S	H	H	H	H	H	HARD HANDS
11	D	D	D	D	D	D	D	D	D	H	
10	D	D	D	D	D	D	D	D	H	H	
9	H	D	D	D	D	H	H	H	H	H	
5-8	H	H	H	H	H	H	H	H	H	H	
A-9	S	S	S	S	S	S	S	S	S	S	
A-8	S	S	S	S	S	S	S	S	S	S	
A-7	S	D	D	D	D	S	S	H	H	H	
A-6	H	D	D	D	D	H	H	H	H	H	
A-5	H	H	D	D	D	H	H	H	H	H	SOFT HANDS
A-4	H	H	D	D	D	H	H	H	H	H	
A-3	H	H	H	D	D	H	H	H	H	H	
A-2	H	H	H	D	D	H	H	H	H	H	
A-A	T	T	T	T	T	T	T	T	T	T	
10-10	S	S	S	S	S	S	S	S	S	S	
9-9	T	T	T	T	T	S	T	T	S	S	
8-8	T	T	T	T	T	T	T	T	T	T	
7-7	T	T	T	T	T	T	H	H	H	H	
6-6	T	T	T	T	T	H	H	H	H	H	PAIRS
5-5	D	D	D	D	D	D	D	D	H	H	
4-4	H	H	H	T	T	H	H	H	H	H	
3-3	T	T	T	T	T	T	H	H	H	H	
2-2	T	T	T	T	T	T	H	H	H	H	

↑
Player's Hand

Note that this book offers just this one Basic Strategy Chart, which covers most casino situations. There are slight nuances to a few of the scenarios on this Basic Strategy chart if (1) it is single-deck game, (2) doubling after splitting is not allowed or (3) the dealer hits on soft 17. However, for the beginner/intermediate player, knowing and using the information in this Basic Strategy chart is quite sufficient for play at the majority of casinos.

Hard Hands

Understanding Hard Hands

- **Hard Total**: A hand without an Ace, or with an Ace valued as 1.
- **Examples**: 10-8 (total 18), 7-6 (total 13), 10-6-A (total 17).

Strategy for Hard Hands

Scenario	Player Action	Reasoning
Hit on Low Totals	Always hit on hard totals of 8 or lower.	You can't bust with a total of 8 or lower, and hitting can only improve your hand.
Double Down on 10 or 11	When your total is 10 or 11 and the dealer's upcard is lower, double down.	A total of 10 or 11 offers a strong chance to draw a 10, resulting in a strong hand. This is an opportunity to maximize your bet and potential profit by doubling.
Stand on High Totals	Stand on totals of 17 or higher.	Hitting on a hard 17 often results in a bust. Even if the dealer shows a 9 or 10, basic strategy indicates that standing is more profitable in the long run.

Soft Hands

Understanding Soft Hands

- **Soft Total**: A hand with an Ace valued as 11.
- **Examples**: Ace-7 (soft 18), Ace-2 (soft 13).

Strategy for Soft Hands

Scenario	Player Action	Reasoning
Hit on Low Soft Totals	Hit on soft totals of 17 or lower.	A hand of 17 or lower is generally weak. If there's a chance to make the hand stronger, you must take it. There's also a chance you will make your hand weaker, but you'll never bust. Never stand with a soft 17 or lower.
Double Down on 13 - 18	Double down on soft totals of 13-18 when the dealer's upcard is favorable.	When the dealer's upcard is a 5 or a 6, it is the most likely to bust. Double down on a soft 13 through 18 to maximize profits. If the dealer is showing a 4, the player is a little less likely to bust, and the player should double down on a soft 15 through 18. Lastly, if the dealer is showing a 3, the dealer is even less likely to bust, and stands a better chance to achieve a 17. The player should only double down on a soft 17 or 18, to achieve a push or edge out a win.
Stand on High Totals	Stand on soft totals of 19 or higher.	A soft 19 or 20 is as good as it gets for a soft hand. If the player takes a hit, the hand will likely remain the same or become weaker. The player would need an ace or a 2 to improve, and the chances are low. Always stand with a soft 19 or 20.

Pairs

Understanding Pairs

- **Splitting Pairs**: When you have two cards of the same value, you have the option to split them into two separate hands.
- **Examples**: 8-8, 7-7.

Strategy for Pairs

Scenario	Player Action	Reasoning
Player hand is A-A or 8-8	**Always split Aces and 8s.**	Splitting Aces gives a strong chance for a winning hand, while splitting 8s turns a weak hand (16) into two potentially stronger hands.
Player hand is 5-5 or 10-10	Never split 5s and 10s.	Treat a pair of 5s as a hard 10 and a pair of 10s as a hard 20, both strong hands that shouldn't be split.
Player hand is 2-2, 3-3 or 7-7	Split 2s, 3s, and 7s when the dealer shows 2-7.	These pairs are weak but can turn into strong hands against a weak dealer upcard, improving your chances of winning both hands.

Strategy for Pairs (cont'd)

Scenario	Player Action	Reasoning
Player hand is 4-4	Split 4s when the dealer shows 5 or 6.	Splitting 4s can turn a total of 8 into potentially stronger hands when the dealer shows a weak 5 or 6 upcard, increasing your chances of winning both hands.
Player hand is 6-6	Split 6s when the dealer shows 2-6.	Splitting 6s turns a total of 12 into potentially winning hands when the dealer has a weak upcard, giving you an opportunity to win two hands instead of just one.
Player hand is 9-9	Split 9s when the dealer shows 2-9 (except 7).	Splitting 9s can turn into strong hands and take advantage of the dealer's weaker upcards, but stand against a 7 to keep a strong total of 18, easily beating the dealer's potential 17.
Other Splits	Evaluate based on specific dealer upcards.	Always check the basic strategy chart for specific splits based on the dealer's upcard, as these can vary and impact your chances of winning.

Surrendering in Blackjack

Surrendering is a strategic option in Blackjack that allows a player to forfeit half of their bet and end their hand immediately after the initial deal. This move is only available as the first decision a player makes, before taking any other actions like hitting, standing, or doubling down. Surrendering can be a smart play in situations where the player's chances of winning are particularly low. The most common scenarios for surrendering are when the player has a hard total of 15 against the dealer's upcard of 10, or a hard total of 16 against the dealer's upcard of 9, 10, or Ace. These hands have a high probability of losing, and surrendering minimizes potential losses. By using the surrender option wisely, players can reduce the house edge and improve their long-term results in Blackjack.

Below is a table summarizing basic strategy in a slightly different, and more intuitive way. Next, several blackjack scenarios will be reviewed, showing the thought process that demonstrates basic strategy.

Surrender	15	vs 10
	16	vs 9, 10, A
Split	2s, 3s, 7s	vs 2-7
	4s	vs 5, 6
	5s & 10s	NEVER
	6s	vs 2-6
	9s	vs 2-9 (except 7)
	As & 8s	ALWAYS
Double (soft)	A2, A3	vs 5,6
	A4, A5	vs 4-6
	A6, A7	vs 3-6
Double (hard)	9	vs 3-6
	10	vs <10
	11	vs <11
Hit (soft)	up to: 18	ALWAYS
Hit (hard)	up to: 13	vs 2, 3
	12	vs 4-6
	17	vs 7 & up

Mnemonic Devices for Memorizing Basic Strategy

Memorizing the basic strategy for Blackjack can be challenging due to the numerous scenarios and decisions involved. Mnemonic devices are memory aids that can help you recall complex information more easily. This chapter will introduce various mnemonic techniques to help you remember the optimal plays in Blackjack without constantly referring to a strategy chart.

Hard Hands Mnemonics

- **Hit on Low Totals (8 or Lower)**

    - **Mnemonic**: "Eight is a Date"
        - **Explanation**: Always hit on hard totals of 8 or lower, as it's like going on a date where you want to improve your chances.
    - **Mnemonic**: "Hit 12-23", or "Hit Twelve-Two-Three"
        - **Explanation**: Always hit a hard 12 against the dealer's 2 or 3.

- **Double Down on 9 against Dealer's 3 through 6**

    - **Mnemonic**: "Double Down on 9 vs 3-6, since 3 + 6 = 9"
        - **Explanation**: When you have a total of 9, double down against the dealer's 3 through 6 because you have a high chance of getting a strong hand.

- **Double Down on 10 or 11 if Dealer shows less**

  - **Mnemonic**: "For Ten and Eleven, When the Dealer is Lower, Double Down and Be Bolder"
    - **Explanation**: When you have a total of 10 or 11, double down against dealer card lower than yours, because you have a high chance of getting a strong hand.

- **Stand on High Totals (Hard 17 or Higher)**

  - **Mnemonic**: "Seventeen is Clean"
    - **Explanation**: Stand on totals of hard 17 or higher, as hitting can often lead to a bust.

Soft Hands Mnemonics

- **Hit on Soft Totals (17 or Lower)**

  - **Mnemonic**: "Soft Seventeen, Hit the Green"
    - **Explanation**: Always hit on soft totals of 17 or lower to improve your hand.

- **Doubling Down**

  - **Mnemonic**: A2, A3 vs 5-6 // A4, A5 vs 4-6 // A6, A7 vs 3-6
    - ○ **Explanation**: There is a pattern on the Basic Strategy Chart for doubling down on soft hands when the dealer shows a weak card. A way to remember this is to repeat to yourself six sets of numbers: "5,6 · 5,6 · 4,5,6 · 4,5,6 · 3,4,5,6 · 3,4,5,6". These pertain to when you should double down on the following six hands: A2, A3 · A4, A5 · A6, A7. The table below demonstrates the relationship:

Soft Hands - Doubling Down

Player's Hand	A2, A3	A4, A5	A6, A7
Dealer's Upcard	5,6	4,5,6	3,4,5,6

- **Stand on Soft Totals (19 or Higher)**

  - **Mnemonic**: "Soft Nineteen, Keep it Clean"
    - ○ **Explanation**: Always stand on soft totals of 19 or higher (A8 or A9) because it's a strong hand that can beat most dealer upcards.

Pairs Mnemonics

- **Always Split Aces and 8s**

  - **Mnemonic**: "Always Split Aces and Eights"
    - ○ **Explanation**: Always split Aces and 8s to maximize your chances of winning.

- **Never Split 5s and 10s**

  - **Mnemonic**: "Fives and Tens, Never Split Again"
    - ○ **Explanation**: Never split 5s and 10s as they form strong hands that shouldn't be divided.

- **Split 2s, 3s, and 7s vs. Dealer's 2-7**

  - **Mnemonic**: "Split 2s, 3s and 7s vs. 2 through 7"
    - ○ **Explanation**: Split 2s, 3s, and 7s when the dealer shows 2-7, as it improves your chances of winning.

- **Split 4s vs. Dealer's 5 or 6**

  - **Mnemonic**: "Split 4s against 5 and 6"
    - ○ **Explanation**: Split 4s when the dealer shows 5 or 6 to take advantage of the dealer's weak upcard.

- **Split 6s vs. Dealer's 2-6**

  - **Mnemonic**: "Split 6s vs. 2 through 6 "
    - ○ **Explanation**: Split 6s when the dealer shows 2-6, as the dealer is likely to bust.

- **Split 9s vs. Dealer's 2-9 (Except 7)**

    - **Mnemonic**: "Seven of Nine" (Sci-fi reference)
        - **Explanation**: Split 9s against dealer's 2-9, except stand on 7 to maximize your chances of winning. Splitting 9s gives you two great first cards to start with, but a starting hand of 18 could easily beat the dealer's 17, and that's why it's best to stand with a pair of 9s when the dealer is showing a 7.

Surrender Mnemonics

- **Surrender 15 vs. 10**

    - **Mnemonic**: "Fifteen against Ten, Surrender then "
        - **Explanation**: Surrender a hard 15 against a dealer's 10 to minimize losses.

- **Surrender 16 vs. 9, 10, or Ace**

    - **Mnemonic**: "Sixteen Against Nine-Ten-Ace, Surrender with Grace "
        - **Explanation**: Surrender a hard 16 against a dealer's 9, 10, or Ace to avoid high chances of losing.

Conclusion

By using mnemonic devices, you can make it easier to remember the basic strategy for Blackjack. These memory aids simplify the complex decisions and help you play optimally without the need for constant reference to strategy charts. Practice these mnemonics regularly to internalize them and improve your gameplay. With enough practice, these rules and all of the basic strategy will become second nature to you.

Chapter 4: Practical Situations Demonstrating Basic Strategy

Introduction

Understanding and applying basic strategy involves recognizing specific situations and knowing the optimal play based on statistical probabilities (all reflected on the Basic Strategy Chart in Chapter 3). This chapter will present practical scenarios to illustrate why certain decisions are recommended. By understanding the reasoning behind these strategies, you can improve your decision-making and increase your chances of winning.

Situation 1: Dealer's Upcard is a 2, and the Player has a Hard 12

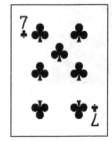 

Basic Strategy Recommendation: Hit

Reasoning: When the dealer's upcard is a 2, the dealer has a relatively neutral hand. The dealer is likely to end up with a total between 8 and 12 after the next card and will be required to hit again. However, the dealer has a reasonable chance of ending up with a strong hand.

For the player, a hard 12 is a precarious hand. Standing on a hard 12 against a dealer's 2 means the player will often lose if the dealer improves their hand beyond 16. Although hitting on a hard 12 carries the risk of busting (drawing a 10-value card), the probability of drawing a card that improves the hand (2 through 9) is greater than the risk of busting.

By hitting, the player has a better chance of improving their hand to a total that can compete more effectively against the dealer's potential hand.

Situation 2: Dealer's Upcard is a 4, and the Player has a Hard 12

Basic Strategy Recommendation: Stand

Reasoning: When the dealer's upcard is a 4, the dealer is in a weak position. The dealer is more likely to bust because they will often end up with a total between 10 and 14 after the next card and will be forced to hit again.

For the player, a hard 12 is still a weak hand, but standing on a hard 12 against a dealer's 4 is statistically advantageous. The reasoning is that the dealer's chances of busting are higher with a 4 showing, and the player does not want to risk busting themselves by hitting.

By standing, the player allows the dealer to play out the hand and hopes the dealer busts, which is a likely outcome given the dealer's weak upcard. This strategy leverages the higher probability of the dealer going over 21, giving the player a better chance of winning the hand.

Situation 3: Dealer's Upcard is a 10, and the Player has a Hard 16

Basic Strategy Recommendation: Surrender (if allowed) or Hit

Reasoning: When the dealer's upcard is a 10, they have a strong chance of achieving a 17 through 20, which is difficult to beat. For the player, a hard 16 is one of the worst hands because it is easy to bust with a hit, but too weak to stand against a strong dealer hand.

If surrender is allowed, it is the best option as it reduces your losses by half. If surrender is not an option, hitting is recommended despite the risk of busting. The reasoning is that hitting gives you a chance to improve your hand to a total closer to 21, which is necessary to compete against the dealer's likely strong hand. The player is most likely to lose this hand, and surrendering averts the risk of losing the entire bet.

Situation 4: Dealer's Upcard is a 6, and the Player has a Soft 18

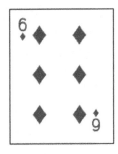

Basic Strategy Recommendation: Double Down

Reasoning: When the dealer's upcard is a 6, the dealer is in a weak position and is more likely to bust. For the player, a soft 18 is a strong hand that can be improved without the risk of busting.

Doubling down in this situation allows the player to increase their bet and take advantage of the dealer's weak position. The probability of the dealer busting or ending up with a weak hand is high, making this an optimal situation to maximize your potential winnings by doubling your bet.

Situation 5: Dealer's Upcard is a 7, and the Player has a Pair of 2s

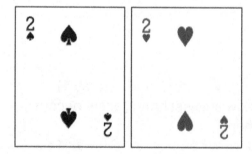

Basic Strategy Recommendation: Split

Reasoning

When the dealer's upcard is a 7, the dealer is in a relatively strong position, likely to end up with a hand total of 17 or higher. The basic strategy recommends splitting a pair of 2s in this situation to improve the player's chances of forming better hands.

Splitting the 2s creates two separate hands, each starting with a 2. This gives the player the opportunity to draw additional cards to each hand and potentially form stronger hands than the initial pair of 2s.

After Splitting:

- **First Hand**: 2
- **Second Hand**: 2

Dealing Additional Cards:

- **First Hand:**
  - Player draws a 7. New hand: 2 and 7 (total: 9). Strategy would now suggest hitting again because 9 is still a weak hand.
  - Player draws a 6. New hand: 2 + 7 + 6 (total: 15). Strategy would now suggest hitting again against the dealer's 7.
  - Player draws a 3. New hand: 2 + 7 + 6 + 3 (total: 18). Strategy would suggest standing as 18 is a strong hand against the dealer's 7.
- **Second Hand:**
  - Player draws a 10. New hand: 2 and 10 (total: 12). Strategy would suggest hitting again because 12 is a weak hand against the dealer's 7.

  - ○ Player draws an 8. New hand: 2 + 10 + 8 (total: 20). Strategy would now suggest standing because 20 is a strong hand.

Possible Outcomes:

- By splitting the pair of 2s, the player creates the potential for stronger hands.
- If one or both hands improve significantly, the player increases the chances of winning against the dealer's 7.

Splitting a pair of 2s against a dealer's 7 is the optimal move according to basic strategy. This approach gives the player two opportunities to build stronger hands and compete more effectively against the dealer's likely strong hand. By following this strategy, players can maximize their chances of success and reduce the house edge in Blackjack.

Situation 5: Dealer's Upcard is a 6, and the Player has a Pair of 4s

Basic Strategy Recommendation: Split

Reasoning

When the dealer shows a 6, it's considered a weak upcard, giving the dealer a higher chance of busting. The player holding a pair of 4s has a total of 8. If the player had a 6-2, the player should take a hit on the hard hand. However, the player has a golden opportunity to potentially maximize profit by creating two hands against the dealer's bust card of 6. Even if the player draws two 10s, and has a weak 14 in each hand, the hope is that the dealer will bust, and the player will win both hands. The splitting approach maximizes the opportunity to win more, as each new hand starts with a 4 and has the chance to build to a higher total through hitting or even doubling down if favorable cards are drawn. It is very possible that after splitting, the player draws a 7, giving a hand of 11, then the player can double down (if allowed after splitting), possibly winning 3 times the initial bet if the dealer busts. Always remember, the end goal of Blackjack is simple:

Conclusion

These practical scenarios demonstrate how basic strategy guides players to make decisions based on the statistical probabilities of different outcomes. By deeply understanding the reasons behind these recommendations, you can make informed decisions that maximize your chances of success at the Blackjack table. Remember, the goal of basic strategy is to minimize the house edge to a minimum and improve the player's odds over the long run.

Lastly, remember to always follow Basic Strategy, even in those situations where your gut tells you not to, and you feel like you're sabotaging your hand. For example, you have a hard 16 against the dealer's 7, and you just "know" you're going to bust by hitting the 16. Just know that based  on the simulations of millions of hands of Blackjack, the expected value and probability all point to hitting the hard 16. In the long run, that gives the player the best edge.

Chapter 5: Advanced Strategies and Tactics

Introduction to Advanced Strategies

Once you have mastered basic strategy, it's time to explore advanced strategies and tactics that can further improve your Blackjack game. This chapter will delve deeper into money management techniques, highlight effective betting strategies, and briefly mention the concept of card counting.

The Reality of Long-Term Play in Blackjack

While Blackjack is a game where skill and strategy can significantly influence outcomes, it's important to acknowledge the mathematical certainty of the house edge. Over a long period of continuous play, this house edge ensures that the casino will ultimately profit, leading to eventual losses for the player (this is why Las Vegas looks like it does). The key to winning at Blackjack lies in recognizing and capitalizing on short-term opportunities when the deck is in your favor. Players must be vigilant, utilizing basic strategy (and perhaps, advanced strategies such as card counting) combined with precise bankroll management to maximize their gains during these favorable periods. However, even the most skilled players should understand that prolonged play increases the likelihood of the house edge eroding their bankroll. To optimize their chances of success, players should focus on short, strategic sessions and know when to walk away, ensuring they preserve their winnings rather than succumbing to the inevitability of long-term losses.

Money Management

Effective money management is crucial in Blackjack. It ensures you can sustain your play over the long term and capitalize on favorable situations. Here are some key principles and strategies for managing your bankroll:

Bankroll Management Principles

- **Set a Budget**: Determine how much money you are willing to risk in a session and stick to it. This prevents you from chasing losses and keeps your gambling fun and within your financial limits.
- **Divide Your Bankroll**: Split your total bankroll into smaller session bankrolls. This allows you to manage your money more effectively and reduces the risk of losing everything in a single session.
- **Set Win and Loss Limits**: Establish win and loss limits for each session. For example, if you double your session bankroll, consider cashing out. Similarly, if you lose a predetermined amount, take a break or end the session.

Calculating the Unit Bet

To manage your bankroll effectively, it's essential to determine a consistent unit bet size. A common guideline is to bet a maximum of 1-2% of your total bankroll on any single hand. This approach minimizes risk and ensures that you can continue playing even after a series of losses. If you're budget is $1,000, consider your unit bet to be $10 - $20

Betting Strategies

Flat Betting

- ○ **Concept**: Bet the same amount on every hand, regardless of wins or losses.
- ○ **Benefits**: This approach is simple and helps manage your bankroll effectively. It reduces the risk of large losses and allows for steady play over time.
- ○ **Drawbacks**: Flat betting does not capitalize on winning streaks, and potential profits are smaller compared to progressive betting systems.

Progressive Betting Systems

1. Martingale System

- **Concept**: Double your bet after each loss to recover losses and make a profit equal to the original bet.
- **Benefits**: Can quickly recover losses and secure a small profit.
- **Drawbacks**: Requires a substantial bankroll and has a high risk of significant losses during a losing streak. Table limits can also prevent you from doubling your bet indefinitely.

Example Scenario for Martingale System

1. **Initial Bet**: $10
2. **First Hand**: Loss, new bet is $20
3. **Second Hand**: Loss, new bet is $40

4. **Third Hand**: Loss, new bet is $80
5. **Fourth Hand**: Win, player wins $80
6. **Total Outcome**: Player lost $10 + $20 + $40 but won $80, resulting in a net profit of $10. The player had to place a bet of $80 just to catch up and be ahead by $10. Losing streaks can be devastating.

2. Paroli System

- **Concept**: The Paroli system, also known as the Reverse Martingale, which involves increasing your bet after each win to capitalize on winning streaks, while returning to your base bet after a loss. The idea is to take advantage of hot streaks and minimize losses during cold streaks.
- **Benefits**: This system can lead to significant profits during a winning streak, as each win compounds your bet size. It also has a built-in loss limitation since you revert to your base bet after a loss, thereby protecting your bankroll.
- **Drawbacks**: The main risk of the Paroli system is that a single loss can wipe out the accumulated profits from previous wins, especially if you are on the third or fourth bet in the progression. Additionally, long losing streaks can still be detrimental to your overall bankroll.

Example Scenario for Paroli System

1. **Initial Bet**: $10
2. **First Hand**: Win, new bet is $20
3. **Second Hand**: Win, new bet is $40
4. **Third Hand**: Win, new bet is $80
5. **Fourth Hand**: Loss, player loses $80
6. **Total Outcome**: Player won $10 + $20 + $40 but lost $80, resulting in a net loss of $10.

In another scenario, if the player wins the fourth hand:

1. **Initial Bet**: $10
2. **First Hand**: Win, new bet is $20
3. **Second Hand**: Win, new bet is $40
4. **Third Hand**: Win, new bet is $80
5. **Fourth Hand**: Win, new bet is $160
6. **Total Outcome**: Player won $10 + $20 + $40 + $80 + $160, resulting in a net profit of $310.

In this system, the key is to set a predefined limit on how many times you will increase your bet after consecutive wins to protect your winnings and avoid the risk of losing them all in a single hand. For example, after three consecutive wins, you might decide to revert to your base bet regardless of the outcome of the next hand. This cautious approach allows you to enjoy the benefits of a modified Paroli system while mitigating its primary risk.

3. Fibonacci System

- **Concept**: The Fibonacci system is a progressive betting strategy based on the famous Fibonacci sequence, where each number is the sum of the two preceding ones (1, 1, 2, 3, 5, 8, 13, …). In this system, you increase your bet according to the sequence after each loss and revert back two steps in the sequence after a win.
- **Benefits**: The Fibonacci system gradually increases bet sizes after losses, reducing the risk of large losses compared to the Martingale system. This method also helps in recovering losses over a series of hands rather than in a single hand, which can make it a more sustainable approach.

- **Drawbacks**: This system requires careful tracking of the sequence and can still lead to significant losses during prolonged losing streaks. Additionally, it may not be suitable for players with limited bankrolls or those playing at tables with low maximum bet limits.

Example Scenario for Fibonacci System

1. **Initial Bet**: $10
2. **First Hand**: Loss, new bet is $10 (next in sequence) [Player lost $10, now -$10]
3. **Second Hand**: Loss, new bet is $20 (next in sequence) [Player loses $10, now -$20]
4. **Third Hand**: Loss, new bet is $30 (next in sequence) [Player loses $20, now -$40]
5. **Fourth Hand**: Win, player wins $30 [Player is now -$10] Move back two steps in the sequence, new bet is $10
6. **Fifth Hand**: Loss, new bet is $10 (next in sequence) [Player loses $10, now -$20]
7. **Sixth Hand**: Loss, new bet is $20 (next in sequence) [Player loses $10, now -$30]
8. **Seventh**: Win, player wins $20 [Player is now -$10] Move back two steps in the sequence, new bet is $10

Total Outcome:

- Losses: $10 + $10 + $20 + $10 + $10 = $60
- Wins: $30 + $20 = $50
- Net Result: $50 - $60 = -$10

In this scenario, despite the player experiencing a series of losses, the Fibonacci system helps to mitigate the overall loss by not escalating the bet size as aggressively as the Martingale system. The player moves back two steps in the sequence after each win, which helps to manage the risk and protect the bankroll over time.

Advanced Example Scenario #1 for Fibonacci System

1. **Initial Bet**: $10
2. **First Hand**: Loss, new bet is $10 (next in sequence) [Player lost $10, now -$10]
3. **Second Hand**: Loss, new bet is $20 (next in sequence) [Player loses $10, now -$20]
4. **Third Hand**: Win, player wins $20 [Player is now +$0] Move back two steps in the sequence, new bet is $10
5. **Fourth Hand**:: Win, player wins $10 [Player is now +$10] Move back two steps (start of sequence), new bet is $10
6. **Fifth Hand**: Loss, new bet is $10 (next in sequence) [Player loses $10. is now +$0]
7. **Sixth Hand**: Loss, new bet is $20 (next in sequence) [Player loses $10, now -$10]
8. **Seventh Hand**: Loss, new bet is $30 (next in sequence) [Player loses $20, now -$30]
9. **Eighth Hand**: Win, player wins $30 [Player is now +$0] Move back two steps in the sequence, new bet is $10

Total Outcome:

- Losses: $10 + $10 + $10 + $10 + $20 = $60
- Wins: $20 + $10 + $30 = $60
- Net Result: $60 - $60 = $0

This more extended sequence shows that while the Fibonacci system can help manage losses and maintain the bankroll better than more aggressive strategies, it still requires careful management and discipline. Players should be aware of table limits and ensure they have enough bankroll to withstand potential prolonged losing streaks.

Let's look at one more example of the Fibonacci System

Advanced Example Scenario #2 for Fibonacci System

1. **Initial Bet**: $10
2. **First Hand**: Loss, new bet is $10 (next in sequence) [Player lost $10, now -$10]
3. **Second Hand**: Loss, new bet is $20 (next in sequence) [Player loses $10, now -$20]
4. **Third Hand**: Win, player wins $20 [Player is now +$0] Move back two steps in the sequence, new bet is $10
5. **Fourth Hand:**: Win, player wins $10 [Player is now +$10] Move back two steps (start of sequence), new bet is $10
6. **Fifth Hand**: Win, player wins $10 [Player is now +$20] Move back two steps (start of sequence), new bet is $10
7. **Sixth Hand**: Loss, new bet is $10 (next in sequence) [Player loses $10, now +$10]
8. **Seventh Hand**: Win, player wins $10 [Player is now +$20] Move back two steps in the sequence, new bet is $10
9. **Eighth Hand**: Win, player wins $10 [Player is now +$30] Move back two steps in the sequence, new bet is $10

Total Outcome:

- Losses: $10 + $10 + $10 = $30
- Wins: $20 + $10 + $10 + $10 + $10 = $60
- Net Result: $60 - $30 = $30

In this particular example, the player follows the Fibonacci betting system and ends up ahead by $30 after 8 hands. The player experiences a couple of early losses but recovers through a series of wins. By adhering to the Fibonacci sequence, the player effectively manages their bets and comes out ahead. This example illustrates how the Fibonacci system can help players capitalize on winning streaks while minimizing losses during losing streaks.

By using the Fibonacci system, players can take a more measured approach to progressive betting, reducing the risk of significant losses while still having the opportunity to recover and make profits over time. However, it can be a bit confusing to track where you are in the betting sequence, and care should be taken when using this system.

4. Labouchere System

- **Concept**: Also known as the Cancellation System, the Labouchere system involves setting a desired profit amount and creating a sequence of smaller numbers that sum to this amount. Bets are made by adding the first and last numbers in the sequence. If the bet wins, those numbers are crossed off; if it loses, the bet amount is added to the end of the sequence.
- **Benefits**: Provides a structured approach to betting and allows for flexibility in setting profit goals. It also offers a clear plan for both winning and losing scenarios.
- **Drawbacks**: Can lead to significant losses during long losing streaks and requires careful tracking of the sequence.

Example Scenario for Labouchere System

1. **Desired Profit**: $50, split into sequence (**10, 10, 10, 10, 10**)
2. **First Bet**: $20 (adding first and last numbers, 10 + 10)
3. **First Hand**: Win, cross off **10** and **10**, new sequence is now (**10, 10, 10**)
4. **Second Bet**: $20 (adding first and last numbers, **10 + 10**)
5. **Second Hand**: Loss, add 20 to the end of the sequence, new sequence is (**10, 10, 10, 20**)
6. **Third Bet**: $30 (**10 + 20**)
7. **Third Hand**: Win, cross off **10** and **20**, new sequence is (**10, 10**)
8. **Fourth Bet**: $20 (**10 + 10**)
9. **Fourth Hand**: Win, cross off **10** and **10**, sequence is complete

Total Outcome:

- Wins: $20 + $30 + $20 = $70
- Losses: $20
- Net Result: $70 - $20 = $50 profit

In this scenario, the Labouchere system helps the player reach the desired profit goal of $50 by following a structured betting plan. Even after a loss, the player continues to bet according to the sequence, eventually achieving the profit target. This system requires discipline and careful tracking but can be effective in managing bets and pursuing profit goals.

By using the Labouchere system, players can systematically approach their betting strategy, ensuring they have a clear plan for both winning and losing scenarios. This structure helps maintain discipline and focus, which are crucial for long-term success in Blackjack.

Brief Mention of Card Counting

Card Counting Basics

- **Concept**: Card counting involves tracking the ratio of high cards to low cards remaining in the deck to predict the likelihood of favorable outcomes.
- **Note**: This book does not cover card counting techniques in detail. Specialized resources and books are available for those interested in mastering card counting. For most players, focusing on basic strategy and money management will provide the best balance of enjoyment and success at the Blackjack table.

Conclusion

Advanced strategies and tactics in Blackjack require practice, discipline, and a deeper understanding of the game's probabilities. By focusing on effective money management and employing strategic betting systems like the Martingale, Paroli, and Fibonacci systems, you can maintain your  bankroll and survive to maintain play. Remember that the key to long-term success in Blackjack is consistency and the ability to manage your bankroll wisely. This disciplined approach will allow you to enjoy the game and increase your chances of coming out ahead.

Chapter 6: Casino Etiquette

Introduction

Understanding and practicing good casino etiquette is crucial for ensuring an enjoyable and respectful environment for all players. Whether you are a seasoned player or a beginner, adhering to the unwritten rules of casino conduct will enhance your experience and that of those around you.

Dress Code

- **Know the Casino's Dress Code**: Some casinos have specific dress codes, especially for high-stakes tables or private rooms. While many casinos are more relaxed, it's always a good idea to dress smartly.

- **Smart Casual**: For most casinos, smart casual attire is appropriate. Avoid overly casual clothing like tank tops, flip-flops, and gym wear.

At the Blackjack Table

- **Wait for the Right Moment**: When joining a table, wait for a natural break in the game, such as when a new shoe is being dealt or between hands. It's also a good idea to spend a few minutes observing the dealer and the gameplay to get a sense of the table's cadence. If you notice that the players are all losing one hand after another and appear miserable, it would be wise to consider finding another table.

- **Buy Chips Politely**: Place your cash on the table and inform the dealer of the amount you wish to exchange for chips. Never hand money directly to the dealer. Cameras above the table are recording every movement and transaction.

- **Know the Signals**: Use hand signals to indicate your decisions:

    o **Hit**: Tap the table with your finger.

    o **Stand**: Wave your hand horizontally.

    o **Double Down or Split**: Place additional chips next to your original bet and use one finger for double down and two fingers for split.

- **Respect the Dealer and Other Players**: Be polite and respectful. Avoid criticizing the dealer or other players, even if the game is not going your way.

Where to Sit

- **First Base**: The first base position is the first seat to the dealer's left. Unless you're solid on basic strategy, it's advisable not to sit here. The first base player acts first after the dealer deals the initial cards, and this can put pressure on you to make quick decisions.

- **Third Base**: The third base position is the last seat to the dealer's right. This position is often considered advantageous because you get to see how all the other players act before making your decision. However, it can also carry the weight of expectations from other players.

- **Middle Positions**: Sitting in one of the middle positions can be less stressful for beginners, as you have more time to consider your actions without the pressure of being the first or last to act.

Handling Chips and Bets

- **Place Bets Carefully**: Place your chips in the designated betting area. Avoid moving or touching your bet once the cards are dealt.

- **Stack Chips Neatly**: Stack your chips in an orderly manner, with higher denomination chips at the bottom.

- **Tip the Dealer**: It's customary to tip the dealer if you're winning. Place a small bet for the dealer or hand them a chip directly.

Do Not Touch the Cards

In a casino Blackjack game, only the dealer handles the cards at the table, and players are generally not allowed to touch them. This rule is in place for several important reasons:

- **Preventing Cheating**

  1. **Security and Integrity**: Allowing only the dealer to handle the cards helps maintain the integrity of the game. It reduces the risk of cheating by preventing players from marking, switching, or manipulating the cards.

  2. **Surveillance**: Casinos use surveillance cameras to monitor gameplay. When only the dealer handles the cards, it simplifies the surveillance process and makes it easier to detect any suspicious activity.

- **Game Speed and Efficiency**

  3. **Consistency**: Dealers are trained to handle the cards quickly and efficiently, ensuring that the game

proceeds at a steady pace. This consistency helps maintain a smooth flow of the game, which is beneficial for both the casino and the players.

4. **Minimizing Disputes**: When players handle the cards, there is a higher likelihood of disputes over card placement or accidental exposure of cards. By having the dealer control the cards, such issues are minimized.

- **Protecting Players**

5. **Reducing Mistakes**: Players who are not accustomed to handling cards in a casino setting might accidentally reveal their cards or make other mistakes that could negatively impact their own game and the game of others at the table.

6. **Fair Play**: Ensuring that only the dealer handles the cards creates a level playing field for all participants. It prevents any player from gaining an unfair advantage through improper card handling.

- **Casino Regulations**

7. **Compliance with Rules**: Casinos operate under strict regulations and guidelines. Part of these regulations includes maintaining control over the cards to prevent any potential violations of gaming laws. Adhering to these rules helps the casino remain in good standing with regulatory bodies.

Managing Drinks and Smoking

- **Keep Drinks Away from the Table**: Place your drink on the cup holders or side tables provided, not directly on the gaming table.

- **Be Considerate When Smoking**: If smoking is allowed, be mindful of where your smoke is going. Use the provided ashtrays and avoid blowing smoke towards other players.

Interacting with Other Players

- **Avoid Giving Unsolicited Advice**: Refrain from offering advice to other players unless they ask for it.

- **Stay Positive**: Keep a positive attitude, even during losing streaks. A good mood can enhance the experience for everyone at the table.

- **Respect Personal Space**: Give other players enough room and avoid touching their chips or cards.

Handling Wins and Losses

- **Celebrate Modestly**: It's fine to celebrate a win, but avoid excessive celebrations that might annoy other players.

- **Handle Losses Gracefully**: Accept losses without complaint. It's part of the game, and maintaining a good attitude is key.

Dealing with Other Players' Reactions

- **Expect Reactions**: If you make a play that doesn't align with basic strategy, other players at the table might say something negative or sneer at you. They may feel that by you either taking a card or not taking a card when you were "supposed to," you will cause them to have a losing outcome or cause the dealer to beat the table.

- **Understand the Deck is Random**: Remember, the deck is completely random, and there is no way to know what's coming next. Someone might say something like "That should have been my Ten!" It's best to just let them talk and concentrate on your own game. Focus on your strategy and enjoy the game, regardless of other players' comments.

- **Ask the Dealer**: If you're ever playing at the table and can't remember what Basic Strategy recommends for a particular hand, you can always ask the dealer for advice at any time. They will let you know what the recommended play is.

Leaving the Table

- **Leave Politely**: When you're ready to leave, wait for a break between hands. Thank the dealer and other players.

- **Cash Out Correctly**: Take your chips to the cashier's cage to exchange them for cash. Do not try to cash out at the table.

Conclusion

Practicing good casino etiquette enhances the gaming experience for everyone involved. By following these guidelines, you can ensure a respectful, enjoyable, and positive atmosphere at the Blackjack table and throughout the casino. Respect, courtesy, and awareness are key to being a valued player in any casino setting.

Chapter 7: Practical Applications and Practice

Introduction

Mastering Blackjack involves not only understanding the strategies and techniques but also applying them effectively in real-world scenarios. This chapter will guide you through practical applications of the strategies you've learned, including practice techniques, dealing with pressure at the table, and using tools to enhance your skills.

Practicing Basic Strategy

Online Simulations and Apps

- **Practice Tools**: Utilize online Blackjack simulations and mobile apps designed to help you practice basic strategy. These tools provide instant feedback on your decisions, helping you learn from mistakes. An excellent free online blackjack simulator can be found at www.wizardofodds.com.
- **Recommended Apps**: Look for highly-rated Blackjack training apps that allow you to customize rules and deck counts to mirror real casino conditions.

Home Practice

- **Card Drills**: Practice with a physical deck of cards. Deal yourself different hands and practice making decisions based on the basic strategy. This helps reinforce your learning and improves your speed in making decisions.
- **Strategy Charts**: Keep a basic strategy chart nearby during practice sessions. Over time, aim to use it less frequently as you become more familiar with the optimal plays.

Dealing with Pressure at the Table

Stay Calm and Focused

- **Mindfulness**: Practice mindfulness techniques to stay calm and focused during gameplay. Deep breathing and visualization can help manage stress and improve concentration.
- **Stick to Strategy**: Trust in the basic strategy you've learned. Avoid making impulsive decisions based on emotions or recent outcomes.

Bankroll Management at the Table

- **Set Limits**: Before starting a session, set clear win and loss limits. Stick to these limits to avoid chasing losses or getting carried away by a winning streak. Be true to your gameplan.
- **Small Bets**: Begin with smaller bets to get comfortable with the table dynamics and dealer. Increase your bets gradually as you gain confidence.

Using Tools to Enhance Skills
Strategy Cards

- **Legal in Many Casinos**: Many casinos allow the use of strategy cards at the table. These cards provide quick reference for optimal plays and can be a useful aid, especially for beginners.
- **Discreet Use**: Use strategy cards discreetly to avoid drawing unnecessary attention.

Betting Systems Apps

- **Track Your Bets**: Use apps designed to help you track your bets and outcomes. These apps can provide insights into your betting patterns and help you refine your strategy.
- **Simulate Different Systems**: Some apps allow you to simulate different betting systems, helping you understand how each system performs over time.

Conclusion

Practical application of the strategies and techniques you've learned is crucial for mastering Blackjack. By practicing regularly, staying calm under pressure, and using tools to enhance your skills, you can improve your gameplay and increase your chances of success at the table. Remember, consistency and discipline are key to long-term success in Blackjack.

Chapter 8: Conclusion

Tying Everything Together

In this book, we have explored the intricate strategies and nuances of playing Blackjack like an engineer. Just as in engineering, success in Blackjack requires a solid foundation in theory, a methodical approach to decision-making, and the ability to adapt to changing conditions.

Learning and Applying Theory

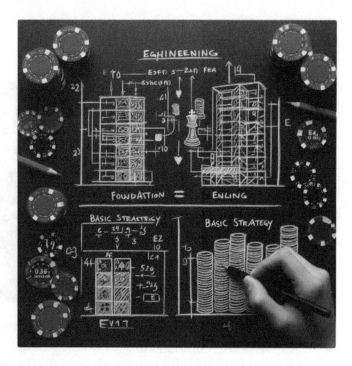

In engineering, students learn proven theories and concepts which they then apply to real-world projects. Similarly, in Blackjack, mastering the basic strategy forms the cornerstone or foundation of success. By understanding and internalizing the rules of the game and the optimal plays, you can approach each hand with confidence, just as an engineer approaches a project with a well-constructed plan.

Project Management and Strategy

Project management in engineering involves meticulous planning, execution, and adjustment based on ongoing assessments. In Blackjack, you must manage your bankroll carefully, make strategic bets, and adjust your play based on the cards dealt and the dealer's upcard. The concept of "for every action, there is a reaction" is fundamental in both fields. In Blackjack, recognizing that the dealer's upcard of 5 or 6 has a high probability of leading to a bust allows you to make informed decisions that maximize your chances of winning.

Budget Management

Budget management is a critical aspect of engineering projects, ensuring that resources are used efficiently and the project stays within financial constraints.

Similarly, in Blackjack, effective bankroll management is essential to sustaining your play and maximizing your long-term profitability. Setting limits, making calculated bets, and avoiding emotional decisions are all part of a disciplined approach that parallels the careful financial oversight required in engineering.

Continuous Improvement

Both engineering and Blackjack are fields where continuous learning and improvement are vital. Engineers stay updated with the latest technologies and methodologies to enhance their work. In Blackjack, continuous practice, staying informed about new strategies, and learning from each playing session help you refine your skills and adapt to different playing environments.

Emotional Control and Discipline

Emotional control is crucial in both engineering and Blackjack. In engineering, staying calm and making rational decisions under pressure can determine the success of a project and the reputation of the engineer. Similarly, in Blackjack, maintaining emotional control, avoiding frustration, and sticking to your strategy regardless of short-term outcomes are key to long-term success and becoming a reputable and respected player.

Parallels in Decision-Making

The decision-making process in Blackjack mirrors that of engineering. Both require analyzing the available information, calculating probabilities, and making the best possible decision to achieve the desired outcome. In Blackjack, understanding the probability of drawing a card with a value of 10 and using that knowledge to guide your actions is akin to an engineer using data and calculations to inform their project decisions.

By integrating these parallels and applying the strategies outlined in this book, you can approach Blackjack with the precision and confidence of an engineer. This methodical approach will enhance your enjoyment of the game and increase your chances of success at the Blackjack table. Remember, the key to excelling in Blackjack, as in engineering, is a combination of knowledge, practice, and disciplined execution. May your strategic approach and discipline lead you to many successful hands at the Blackjack table!

Engineering and Blackjack

Glossary of Blackjack Terms

Ace: A card that can be worth either 1 or 11 points, depending on which value is more favorable for the player's hand.

Action: The total amount of money wagered by a player in a betting session.

Blackjack: A hand consisting of an Ace and a 10-value card (10, Jack, Queen, or King), totaling 21 points. Also known as a "natural."

Bust: A hand that exceeds 21 points, resulting in an automatic loss for the player or dealer.

Card Counting: A strategy used to keep track of the ratio of high to low cards remaining in the deck to predict the likelihood of favorable outcomes. This book does not cover card counting techniques in detail.

Double Down: An option for the player to double their initial bet in exchange for committing to stand after receiving exactly one additional card.

Even Money: A payout of 1:1 on a player's winning bet. For example, a $10 winning bet would result in a $10 profit.

Face Card: Any Jack, Queen, or King card, each worth 10 points.

Hard Hand: A hand that does not contain an Ace, or if it does, the Ace counts as 1 point to avoid busting.

Hit: The action of requesting an additional card to be added to the player's hand.

Hole Card: The dealer's face-down card, revealed only after all players have completed their actions.

Insurance: A side bet offered when the dealer's upcard is an Ace, allowing players to bet on the dealer having a blackjack. It pays 2:1 if the dealer has a blackjack.

Natural: Another term for blackjack, a hand totaling 21 points with an Ace and a 10-value card.

Push: A tie between the player's hand and the dealer's hand, resulting in no win or loss for the player.

Soft Hand: A hand that contains an Ace counted as 11 points without busting. For example, an Ace and a 6 would be a soft 17.

Split: The action of dividing a pair of cards of the same value into two separate hands, each with its own bet, after which the player can hit, stand, or double down as usual.

Stand: The action of ending the player's turn without taking any additional cards.

Surrender: An option for the player to forfeit half of their bet and end their hand early. This option is not available in all casinos.

Upcard: The dealer's face-up card, visible to all players.

Wager: The amount of money bet on a hand of blackjack.

Author's Bio

David A. Janover, PE, F.NSPE, CFM

David A. Janover, PE is a seasoned professional engineer and former adjunct professor with a passion for both engineering and the game of Blackjack. With over 30 years of experience in civil engineering, David has applied his analytical skills and strategic thinking to enhance the experience and enjoyment of the game of Blackjack, and is eager to share these concepts with the reader. David earned both his Bachelor's and Master's degrees in Civil Engineering from The Cooper Union in New York City.

David's engineering career spans the private and public sectors, with the last 23 years as a public servant, including his current role as the Town Engineer for a municipality in Arizona. His methodical approach to problem-solving and project management has earned him a reputation for excellence in his field.

Combining his engineering expertise with his love for Blackjack, David has developed unique strategies that bridge the gap between technical analysis and gaming. His systematic approach to Blackjack, detailed in this book, reflects his belief that the principles of engineering can be effectively applied to mastering the game.

To reach out to David, please send an email to djanover1@gmail.com.